GW01085834

THE BIG GREEN POETRY MACHINE

Amazing Poets

Edited By Allie Jones

First published in Great Britain in 2023 by:

Young Writers
Remus House
Coltsfoot Drive
Peterborough
PE2 9BF
Telephone: 01733 890066
Website: www.youngwriters.co.uk

Printed and bound in the UK by BookPrintingUK
Website: www.bookprintinguk.com
YB0542HZ

FOREWORD

Welcome Reader,

For Young Writers' latest competition The Big Green Poetry Machine, we asked primary school pupils to craft a poem about the world. From nature and environmental issues to exploring their own habitats or those of others around the globe, it provided pupils with the opportunity to share their thoughts and feelings about the world around them.

Here at Young Writers our aim is to encourage creativity in children and to inspire a love of the written word, so it's great to get such an amazing response, with some absolutely fantastic poems. It's important for children to be aware of the world around them and some of the issues we face, but also to celebrate what makes it great! This competition allowed them to express their hopes and fears or simply write about their favourite things. The Big Green Poetry Machine gave them the power of words and the result is a wonderful collection of inspirational and moving poems in a variety of poetic styles.

I'd like to congratulate all the young poets in this anthology; I hope this inspires them to continue with their creative writing.

NATURE WILDLIFE INSECTS EARTH RECYCLE

CONTENTS

Owen Stancliffe (9) 64
Mia Barrett (8) 65
Luke Harris (9) 66
Austin Eastwood (8) 67
Seren Dorrington (9) 68
Jacob Cheeseman (8) 69

Oak Field Primary School, Gibbonsdown

Maliyah-Rae Brown (8) 70
Alieu-Ieuan Bah (8) 71
Taya-May Jones (8) 72
Alfie Way (8) 73
Theo Welch (8) 74
Rosanna Spragg (8) 75
Brooklyn Bennett (9) 76
Georgia Dudley (9) 77
Lloyd Crump (8) 78
Romeo Hawker (9) 79
Melissa Rowlands (8) 80

Ralph Butterfield Primary School, Haxby

Archie Walton (6) 81
Finley Smith 82
Annabelle Smith (6) 83
Jacob Humphrey (6) 84
Emma Gillah (6) 85
Lucy Kumar (6) 86
Maggie Gray (7) 87
Annabel Cameron (7) 88
Evie Dickinson (7) 89
Maisie Gott (6) 90
Kuba Madhavan (6) 91
Joe Thompson (6) 92
Hazel Atherton (6) 93
Ruby Walton (6) 94
Thomas Elsom (7) 95
Thomas Crundwell (7) 96
Sophia Dodsworth (6) 97
Jay Madhavan (6) 98
Oliver Ryan (6) 99

Amy Saidykhan (6) 100
Autumn Bodden (6) 101
Noah Thorpe (7) 102
Emily Frank (7) 103
Chester Bell (6) 104
Vinnie Varley (6) 105
Tess Holliday (6) 106
William Greaves (6) 107
Noah Wardell (5) 108
Alfie Ward (5) 109
Olivia Strange (6) 110
Martha Arbon (5) 111
Freya Boothman (7) 112
Kyrah Amaral (6) 113
Molly Thrower (7) 114
Lucas Newton-Bacon (7) 115
Martha Clark (7) 116
Max Snow (7) 117
Esmée Wilkins Raw (6) 118
Millie Macfarlane (6) 119
Jack Evans (7) 120
Esmae Read (6) 121
Jacob Wright (6) 122
Harry Sturdy-Evans (5) 123
Scarlett Turner (6) 124
Emily Elsom (5) 125

Richard Whittington Primary School, Bishop's Stortford

Rhea Butwell (10) 126
Noah Groom (10) 127
Paige Gamble (10) 128
Teodor Bosca (10) 129
Maisie Hicking (10) 130
Emily Beaufond (10) 131
Will Bennett 132
Andrew Randle (10) 133
Kai Lumley (10) 134
Harlie Stewart (10) 135
Ottilai Jermy (10) 136
Lily Springate (10) 137
Sonnie Lynch (10) 138
Kieran Dedman (10) 139

Sam Jones (10)	140
Elly-May Robertson (10)	141
Aaya El-Sharkawy (10)	142
Aleksandra Dopcheva (10)	143
Ryan Thomson (10)	144

St John's CE Primary Academy, Stafford

Lucas Rogers (10)	145
Ellie Booth (9)	146
Devansh Pun (9)	147
Thomas Wright (10)	148
Ethan Harley (10)	149
Bella Langford (9)	150
Phoebe Bull (10)	151
Leah Sinclair (10)	152
Marvin Limbu (9)	153
Alona Shinu (10)	154
Sarah Wright (10)	155
Anusha Gurung (9)	156
Ernie Kenderdine (10)	157
Thomas Devine (10)	158
Charlie Grantham (10)	159
Arthur Sutton (9)	160

Wix & Wrabness Primary School, Wix

Annabel John (9)	161
Leon Fulljames (9)	162
Felicity Randall (10)	164
Anise Arthey (9)	165
Thomas Mackintosh (8)	166
Mason Hicks (9)	167
Madison Kindred (10)	168
Dolly Demi Lucas Angus (9)	169
Erin Philipson (9)	170
Rueben Smith (10)	171
Jacob Boswell (7)	172
Laney Gansbuhler (10)	173
Sammy Fenton (8)	174
Thomas Thornicroft (8)	175
Phoenix Hasson (9)	176

Finn Muldoon (8)	177
Neve Poppy Cansdale (8)	178
Holly Vincent (9)	179
Robert Kindred (8)	180
Lydia Thornton (9)	181
Freya Good (9)	182
Thomas Burls (8)	183
Harry Spence (9)	184
Finley Bartlett (9)	185
Oliver Walmsley (9)	186
Millie Robb (7)	187
Evana Hughes (8)	188
Mason Bartlett (7)	189
Mason Walmsley (7)	190
Adam Lee (7)	191
Erin Barker (8)	192
Billy Spence (7)	193
Ryan Smith (9)	194
Coen Smith (7)	195
Romeo Thursting (7)	196
Jake Grimwood-Murray (7)	197
Ellie Oldroyd (7)	198
Harrison Houlton (8)	199
Dylan Thorndike (7)	200
Rocco Smith (7)	201

Woodbury Salterton CE Primary, Woodbury Salterton

Megan Wickins (11)	202
Ivy Regan (8)	204
Luca Ficken (10)	205
Tessa Wickins (9)	206
Olivia Drake (10)	207
Brodie Nosworthy (11)	208
Skyla Melluish (10)	209
Florence Robinson (8)	210
Alice Gillies (9)	211
Joff Rorke (10)	212
Kyle Johnston (11)	213
Frank Rorke (8)	214
Henry Haines (11)	215

THE POEMS

The Giant Panda

Through the silvery mist of the mountain,
The coal-black-eyed panda roams,
Searching solitary for the bamboo shoots
That nourish her furry frame.

Rolling joyfully on the snow-covered ground,
Wearing a frosty-white and inky-black coat.
It hides her amongst shady trees and snowy
leaves,
And warms her against the biting cold.

Cradling her tiny, helpless cub,
Enveloping like a winter night,
Emerging when he's strong enough,
To face the springtime sunshine's glare.

Playfully, they clamber over steel-grey rocks,
He scampers skyward up a tree,
She pulls him down gently with her powerful jaws,
Back to the safety of the sunlit earth.

Hugo Cervera-Jackson (9)
Cameron Vale School, London

Tiger's Terrible Disaster!

Tiger, tiger shining bright.
Home in the forest day and night.
Trees will glow and he will flow.
He will retire from the fire.
What's this nonsense after all?

'Twas a burning, glowy night,
And that's the time he will fight.
What, the hands seized the fire!
And what will happen to the tiger?

Will he ever prance again?
Will he ever run insane?
What we'll see is pain inside his vein.
What will happen to the tiger?

Poor little tiger has pain!
All of this mess is stuck in his brain.
Sadness tucked in one place.
Everything is burning in his face.
And that's the time he began to faint.
What will happen to the tiger?

The tiger's cage is a fire pit,
The tiger began to dance and shout for help!
A boy appeared from the shouting he could hear.
He saved the tiger and his place.

Tiger, tiger, shining bright.
Peace at last in the forest day and night.
You should team up with me right now.
Let's save this world together now!

Eva Sugrobova (10)
Cameron Vale School, London

The Red Squirrel

With tired eyes,
She fondly said her goodbyes,
Mysteriously the red squirrel ran and ran,
This task she had to do as fast as she can.

Without a sound she crept away,
This was her secret where she'd play
As quickly as she could she ran up a tree,
And looked up at the vibrant sea.

Between the towering trees,
She could feel the powerful breeze,
Under cloudless skies,
She could see her supplies.

After some time, she decided to climb,
Her favourite tree, the old Scotch pine,
She ran over one hundred metres,
And ran as fast as the cheetahs.

Robin Clake (8)
Cameron Vale School, London

The Lion

Thy light-hearted lion was standing on
Thy mighty mountain with pride
Watching the river tide.
Thy light-hearted lion was standing on
Thy mighty mountain
Waiting to feast on his prey
Every second his mouth was watering with decay.
Thy light-hearted lion was
Cowering in fear
While staying away from the blazing forest fire
Praying in great horror.
Thy dark-hearted lion was standing
With sorrow on a rock that was smashed and
shattered
Thy food, thy river, all laid to waste...

Caleb Armah (11)
Cameron Vale School, London

Scottish Wild Cat

S kinning birds,
C unning cat,
O n the move,
T errific talons,
T wirling tails,
I n the woods,
S niffing around, silent hunter,
H unting prey.

W oodland cat, Highland tiger,
I would love to see you
L icking your kittens,
D oing your prowling at dawn and dusk each day.

C aptive cat now,
A nd you are almost extinct,
T oday, I've written this poem for you.

John Clake (6)
Cameron Vale School, London

Our Wonderful Reef

Suddenly, our underwater world has lost its colour,
Where there was coral there is now blank space,
With no more home, the angelfish gave each other
an embrace.
No more time to race
For the best coral space.

We must save the world at great pace.
So open the gates, the sea awaits.

Scientists warn.
The sea is too warm.
We need a solution,
To stop the pollution.

Elisabeth Forsyth (9)
Cameron Vale School, London

Red Squirrels

Mysteriously the shiny, awe-inspiring red squirrel
Liked looking at the black-as-a-bin shiny beetle
Calm-looking red squirrel curiously looking for
acorns
Other squirrels found their precious food and
started to scorn
Under cloudless skies, the red squirrel family could
see the sunrise
The soft fluffy creature gazing drearily at the rising
sun with its coal-black eyes.

Kamil Bonnier (8)

Cameron Vale School, London

Save The Penguins

P enguins waddling across slippery ice with cute babies.

E xcept for the hunting ones in the cold, rising sea.

N othing is going well, in fact they're a little endangered.

G ood not coming quick enough.

U nable to do anything.

I ce caps are melting rapidly.

N ow we can stop this.

S ave the penguins.

George Mall-Beresford (7)

Cameron Vale School, London

Small Badger

S couting at night
M arking my spot
A cting brave
L ifting mud
L ong sitting

B iting insects
A ctive hunter
D iving for insects
G uarding my space
E ating insects
R epetitive running.

Ralph Forsyth (7)

Cameron Vale School, London

Bunnies

So cute they play
They run away
They're all cosied up
They will not wake up.

They have to eat
Never eat meat
They're so snuggly
Like a cuddly.

They are so cute
Love carrot root
Their ears are so long
Their cuteness is so strong.

Sadie Jackson (9)
Cameron Vale School, London

11

Baby Elephants

Baby elephants like to roll in the mud,
Playing with their bud.
Their ears flap to keep them cool,
And they love to drink from the watering hole.
But if there's too much heat and little rain,
They will die and we won't see them again!

Charlotte Keeley (9)
Cameron Vale School, London

Big Badger

B iting insects
I nsect eating
G rrr, badger

B iting animals
A ctive hunter
D igging insects
G rrr, badger
E ating insects
R unning quickly.

Rafi Bonnier
Cameron Vale School, London

Endangered Tigers

Stripy skin
Prowling at night
Growling and snarling
Antelope for lunch
Glaring eyes
Creeping camouflage
Pouncing and leaping
Tigers endangered
Habitats destroyed.

Manos Markogiannakis (7)
Cameron Vale School, London

Save The Pygmy Sloths

Haiku poetry

Pygmy sloths are friends
Why do we keep them in zoos?
Let's stop cutting trees.

Let's be cuddly now
Donate to save the soft sloths
Big arms mean big hugs.

Alexander Staff (8)
Cameron Vale School, London

Planes

P lanes fly high
L ook at the clouds
A bird flies by
N ow we have to land
E verybody gets off
S ee you soon.

Theodor Wennberg (5)

Cameron Vale School, London

Big Fox

B aking cakes
I cing buns
G reen garden

F or things to eat
O range fur
X -ray vision.

Axel Carlsson (6)

Cameron Vale School, London

Aaaannndd It's Tuesday

Our wee mouse's name was a day of the week,
He loved to play hide-and-seek,
There was a nail,
Stuck on his tail!
He wailed and wailed,
While it hailed!
He met up with a friend,
Who lived around the bend,
The farmer cried,
While the pancakes fried.
He met Wednesday the mouse,
They went to his house,
He went for a steak with a friend,
Who knew where it would end?
Who started a fight,
Who knew his might?
The grave was a mound,
A pile on the ground,
Uh-oh, there's a cat,
Who chased a rat,

His funeral was miserable,
Which made them all vulnerable,
Hey, hey, hey,
There might be a way,
To bring him back to life,
Because he has a wife,
A true love's kiss,
Would be gone in a bliss,
There were seven mouses,
Who lived in nice houses,
His house was so black,
Yes, he was back.

Eilidh Campbell (10)
Darvel Primary School, Darvel

Friday The Brown Mouse

Friday the brown mouse
Ran through the brown house
Yes, these are days of the week
They like to play hide-and-seek
There was a nail
Stuck in his pink tail
He met up with a mouse
Who had a nice house
Friday planned a flight
And went to see a mouse with bad eyesight
He went to sleep
And his dad began to sweep
The mouse's double
Got into trouble
He went to save him
But found a mouse called Tim
He asked him
About a mouse named Glim
He said he didn't know
But gave him a bow
Tim received an invite

Which gave him a fright
Friday's funeral was miserable
Which made him vulnerable
Tim knew Friday had gone away
But his flight was due for a delay.

Callie Park (10)

Darvel Primary School, Darvel

The Wee Brown Mouse

Kyle the mouse had a cheeky grin
He loved to rummage through the black bin
The little mouse was covered in mats
He was always chased by the brown cat
The mouse was a very dark black
He loved to eat a double Big Mac
While running he fell down a drain
He was crying and in a lot of pain
He got back up and ran through the drain
He saw the Grim Reaper and ran away
He made it back up and jumped in the bin
He found some wrapping paper and wrapped his
limb
The wee black mouse was getting hungry
He saw a field and drank some honey
He saw the king bee and ran off in a hurry
When he got home it was blurry.

Kyle Jess (10)
Darvel Primary School, Darvel

The Big Brown Mouse

The big brown mouse had a cheery grin
He loved rambling in the black bin
The big brown mouse was really speedy
He was also really, really greedy
The big brown mouse rampaged in the town
He was really white and really brown
The big brown mouse saw a huge nail
Then unfortunately it stabbed on his tail
The big brown mouse was in a lot of trouble
Oh no where was he? In a big pile of rubble
The big brown mouse was really pale
Poor brown mouse, he was really frail
He jumped really high off the ground
When he landed he was round
He really had a great fright
He started to become very white.

Callan McQuade (10)
Darvel Primary School, Darvel

Danger Mouse

The big brown mouse had to zoom,
So that he could be groomed,
The red curtain was bitten by a kitten,
With strangely shaped mittens,
The little mouse was always in trouble,
And he would always hide in the rubble,
The cat would always chase his tail,
And when he bit it he would let out a wail,
The mouse's tummy would always rumble,
And when it rumbled the ground crumbled,
The poor homeless cat,
Was the complete opposite of fat,
The small mouse would always look in the bin,
In the hope of finding a tin,
The mouse was very frail,
Because he had no tail.

Charlie Wellby (10)
Darvel Primary School, Darvel

Lilac's Adventure

The wee mouse stood on a nail,
While running around in the hail,
Then a little man stood on her tail,
Somehow she fell into the mail,
A man hit her with a broom,
While she was hiding in the room,
She now knew it was time to zoom,
Until boom and crash, crash and boom,
Then Lilac met a friend,
Who said she'd be there until the end,
Lilac knows when she lies,
And knows their friendship is a disguise,
And all Milly wants is a prize,
However, Lilac is very wise,
Lilac thinks Milly is silly,
But Till doesn't know what she thinks of Milly.

Robyn Speirs (10)
Darvel Primary School, Darvel

Wednesday The White Mouse

My pet mouse is white
And has bad eyesight
There is a nail
Around her tail
Her name is Wednesday
But she is not like any other day
She let out a shriek
When they played hide-and-seek
When they were playing hide-and-seek
There was a big leak
We saw a cat and the house
So I instantly picked up my mouse
I went to the house
With my mouse
Me and my mouse sat on the bed
We got fed on the bed
Me and my mouse fell asleep
That is what we did for a week
And for a week we also played hide-and-seek.

Holly Strang (10)
Darvel Primary School, Darvel

The Wee Brown Mouse

A wee brown mouse lived in rubble,
Because he caused a lot of trouble,
The rubble was in a big, big town,
The wee brown mouse had a big frown,
The wee brown mouse went to get some cheese,
The wee brown mouse said, "Can I get this cheese please?"
The wee brown mouse saw a bin,
He was being chased so he hid in a tin,
Someone stepped on his tail,
He let out a big loud wail,
He met a mouse called Kyle,
They sat down and chatted for a while.

Logan Bowerbank (10)
Darvel Primary School, Darvel

The Wee Mouse

The wee mouse was very thin
His wee home was in the bin
The wee mouse had a frown
He was the fastest in town
The wee mouse was very fat
He always got chased by a cat
The little brown mouse had a long tail
It was as sharp as a big long nail
The little mouse ran on the ground
He went on the roundabout and went around
The poor wee mouse, oh no, he got rumbled
They flung him out and he tumbled and tumbled.

Alfie Richmond (10)
Darvel Primary School, Darvel

The Wee Mouse

The wee mouse stood on a nail,
While running around in the hail,
Then a man stood on his tail,
Somehow he slid into the mail,
Then he let out a big wail,
Then he went home with a snail,
He will not stand on the mouse's tail,
If he does he will go to jail,
The man did not want to go,
So he said no,
The man's name was Joe,
Then the man found a doe,
Then he said, "Yo yo yo!"

Chloe Lennon (10)
Darvel Primary School, Darvel

My Mouse

A little brown mouse came into town,
Along came a girl called Abby Brown.
He splattered all over the ground,
Unfortunately, he was round.
His tail looked like a squished nail,
Then a cat came along and sat on the mail.
The little mouse looked very pale,
He thought he was going to fail.
He started to wail,
What shivered? His tail,
And he was so frail.
And that was the end of his long day!

Abby Brown (10)
Darvel Primary School, Darvel

The Sneaky Mouse

The sneaky mouse loved to groom,
But once he was finished he needed to zoom,
As he zoomed he had a big grin,
And what did he see? A black bin,
In the bin he found a nail,
And somehow stabbed his tail.
Oh, poor mouse, he rolled all around,
He was so hurt, he fell on the ground,
The mouse was so frail,
He started to look pale.

Jacob Starritt (11)
Darvel Primary School, Darvel

31

The Mouse

The mouse had a big tail
His favourite thing was a white and black whale.

The wee sneaky brown and white mouse
Was in the town and found a house.

The mouse got chased by a big black cat
But the mouse could not get away because it was fat.

The cat was so hungry and thin
The cat had to find food in the bin.

Rhys Wilson (10)
Darvel Primary School, Darvel

The Brown Mouse

The wee brown mouse is very small
He likes to run but he would always fall
The wee brown mouse was chased by a cat
He cannot get away because he is fat
It did not help that it caught his tail
Because there was a big sharp nail
He was in very big trouble
He was scared and crumbled...

Ava Wilson (10)
Darvel Primary School, Darvel

The Greatest Mouse

The greatest mouse
Was running around the lady's house
He was trying to find some food in her bin
Because he was very, very thin
Instead the mouse slipped on the mat
Which meant he slipped into the cat
The rat was big and brown
He had a big crown.

Jay Robertson (10)
Darvel Primary School, Darvel

The Greedy Mouse

The mouse was brown,
But with a gold crown,
The mouse was very speedy,
And very greedy,
The little mouse,
Was in his big house,
The mouse was so fat,
He couldn't run from the cat,
He hurt his tail,
Because it got stuck on a nail.

Owen Verner (10)
Darvel Primary School, Darvel

The Mouse

The cat got hit by a bat
The mouse sat on the mat
The cat sat on a bean
The mouse's house was very clean
The wee sleek rat heard a loud sound
The mouse had a big bounce
Then the wee mouse saw a whale
The fat mouse went out in a gale.

Alfie Walker (10)

Darvel Primary School, Darvel

The Little Tired Mouse

The little tired mouse
Lived in a house
And the cat would always pounce
When he saw the mouse
So the tired mouse hid in a bowl
But the mouse would always hit a pole
But one day he fell in coal
Trying to run from the pole.

Caiden Watson (11)
Darvel Primary School, Darvel

Bobby The Brown Mouse

Bobby the brown mouse
He lived in a small house
Bobby was really, really thin
He had to look for food in the bin
Bobby's tail was caught in a nail
Bobby got sick and he turned pale.

Brodie Higgins (10)
Darvel Primary School, Darvel

Change The Wrong To Right

Our Earth is all about flowers that bloom,
Not about being in doom.
Our Earth is all about animals and wildlife,
But instead the atmosphere is being cut by a knife.
Together we can make a change,
Maybe by using bikes and going on hikes.
Together we can make a change,
We can help fish that live silently under the sea.
We could be the ones to set them free.
The breaking down of trees,
Is destroying the bees and monkeys.
We need to save them from extinction today,
Because if not we will pay.
Habitats are being destroyed,
And this is something we have to avoid.
We can change the wrong to right.

Lorrae-Trace Randell (10)

Engaines Primary School & Nursery, Little Clacton

How To Help The Environment

S o you want to help the planet
A nd you want some new ideas
V arious things can be done
E veryone can do something, have no fear

T rees are important, they absorb CO_2
H elp by planting new ones and
E nsure we protect the animals that are only a select few

P lease recycle where you can
L eave everything in the right bin
A void using wet wipes and single plastic, now there's a plan
N ow travel by walking or cycling
E at more vegetables rather than meat as well
T urn off your devices to save electricity, to others tell

N ow is the time to take action

O r else it may be too late

W e are surrounded by nature and we decide its fate.

Freya Veale (7)

Engaines Primary School & Nursery, Little Clacton

The Terrific Turtles

T urtles are a type of reptile known as testudines

U nder the sand is where turtles lay eggs and cover them to keep them warm so they can hatch

R escuing turtles will rapidly increase their population and prevent them from being critically endangered and hunted

T urtles rarely leave the ocean, apart from when females come ashore to lay their eggs

L ots of turtle eggs get eaten by predators like hawks, seagulls and toucans

E xotic creatures like turtles are already endangered and we need to start helping them or they will go extinct.

Eddie Everett (10)

Engaines Primary School & Nursery, Little Clacton

Save The Planet

Wiggle your toes, nose and fingers
And make them linger
Because I dream
Of cleaning out the streams
Stop killing the world, the beautiful one
The one you're on because we're nearly done
Recycle your rubbish
Because you are killing animals
Pollution is killing us
And we need to stop at once
We need to care about us, plants and the air
Climate change is melting the ice with every slice
Every moment the Earth is hot or cold
Help us please!
Save the planet!

Jorja Russell (6)
Engaines Primary School & Nursery, Little Clacton

All About Me!

I come from Madagascar, but you can find me in
some zoos
I have bright orange eyes
I am grey and black and white in colour
I love to climb and play
I'm an endangered species of animal
People hunt me for food, the pet trade and
humans are destroying my home!
If you don't look after us, my friends and I may
become extinct!
What am I?

Answer: A ring-tailed lemur.

Phoebe Root (9)
Engaines Primary School & Nursery, Little Clacton

Help The Rainforest

R espect the forest always

A lways throw your rubbish away

I nstead of leaving your rubbish on the ground, pick it up

N ever cut down trees for

F un

O h respect the things around you

R ecycle all you can

E verything should be recycled

S end your love to the forest

T ype 'how to get a job helping the forest'.

Freya Hanson (7)

Engaines Primary School & Nursery, Little Clacton

Wake Up!

Too many cars
Too much waste
Not enough changes
Helping our race

Rainforests that die
Pollution in our sea
What will it take
For our nation to agree?

A change needs to happen
We need to wake up
Destroying our planet
For greed and a buck

We all play a part
But what is yours?
Go and help
But don't sit indoors.

Lottie Little (8)
Engaines Primary School & Nursery, Little Clacton

The Little Dancing Frog

I saw a little frog
He was dancing on a log
He did a spin
And ended up going for a swim
Then he was eaten by a fish
The fish started dancing with a croak in this throat
Out popped the frog, spinning and twirling
To the sound of the splash and splish
Of the fish
Dancing in the water
Under the stars of the midnight sky.

Mya Sneddon (7)

Engaines Primary School & Nursery, Little Clacton

Save Our Dolphins

D on't throw your rubbish in the sea

O ceans are homes for dolphins

L ittering is bad!

P lastic is supposed to go in the bin

H elp the community

I am important, just like you

N o one deserves to live like this

S o help our planet, together we can make a change.

Brooke Wilkins (7)
Engaines Primary School & Nursery, Little Clacton

Koala Bears

Cute and cuddly
Fluffy and lovely
Australia is my country
Does this make me lucky?

Climbing trees
Eating eucalyptus leaves
Sleeping and drinking all day
These are my favourite things

Destruction and disaster
Bush forest fire
Makes me sad
Makes me mad.

Evie Konninge (6)
Engaines Primary School & Nursery, Little Clacton

The Ocean

The ocean is big, the ocean is blue
We must protect nature and the environment too.
To help Planet Earth, recycle what you use
Put plastic in the bin, not in the sea
So our dreams of saving Earth can become a
reality.

Issy Devaux (7)
Engaines Primary School & Nursery, Little Clacton

Save The Environment

Forests, flowers, insects,
Home of all animals,
All of them are beautiful,
But there is a problem,
Everybody is cutting down trees,
And ruining our environment,
So let's team up,
And help nature.

Ecrin Tarac

Engaines Primary School & Nursery, Little Clacton

Protect Nature

Nature is wild
Wild is life
Plant some trees
Water some seeds
Don't interrupt the wildlife
Leave them to what they do
Butterflies fly around the world
And remember
Don't cut down trees!

Aaliyah Stroud (8)
Engaines Primary School & Nursery, Little Clacton

The Red Pandas

R are
E ndangered
D on't touch

P ointed ears
A gile
N ervous
D inky
A crobatic
S nuggly!

Mia Hill (9)

Engaines Primary School & Nursery, Little Clacton

Help The Earth

H elp the environment
E verybody clean up rubbish around the world
L eaping frogs climb trees
P rotect and save trees.

Chanel Curl (7)

Engaines Primary School & Nursery, Little Clacton

Sharks Need Help

S ave sharks so they don't go extinct
H elp them survive, eat and drink
A lways proceed to help sharks
R emember that some sharks are rare
K illers or not killers, we still need to help
S adly, not enough people help, they kill

H ard for us to keep them alive
E ven though it's hard we need to help
L isten for the right time to help sharks
P lease help sharks, they don't deserve this treatment

N ever stop trying to help sharks
E ver feel like giving up, well don't, try to help
E at, drink won't do a thing to sharks
D ull people don't help, but you can
E ating fish is what sharks do, but they don't eat you
D on't ever kill sharks.

Max Summers (9)
Norton CE Primary School, Norton

YoungWriters® Est. 1991

The Seven Days Of God

T he world is where we live
H elp the animals
E verybody should help

S o can you help?
E verything should have a home
V enus is not the place, or any other planet
E verything has a right to live
N ever let this happen

D o oil trees provide oxygen?
A fter the plants are gone, what will provide oxygen?
Y ou need to help
S o will you stop?

O ffer to help
F ind hope in the world

G od left us the world to protect
O il trees won't help
D on't leave me waiting.

Owen Sutcliffe (9)
Norton CE Primary School, Norton

Rainforest

R ainforest trees are being cut down

A nimals' homes are being destroyed

I n the rainforest, everything's going

N o one is doing anything about this

F orest friends are going to be homeless

O n the rainforest floor will stand nothing if we don't help

R eplant trees where the old ones were cut down

E very animal's home is going to be gone without our help

S top cutting down trees if you want to help

T rees will not survive without our help.

Daisy Sawkins (9)

Norton CE Primary School, Norton

Beautiful Nature

B elieve we can change

E co-friendly

A nimals are dying

U tterly horrible

T rees falling

I nstead of resting

F ight for the trees

U nder your feet there are seeds growing

L ove them and water them too

N ature is dying

A nimals are losing their homes

T here are so many things we can do

U nder the trees you are standing, watching them die

R ainforests are falling

E arth is dying.

Jack Page (8)

Norton CE Primary School, Norton

Save The Trees

D on't cut down trees
E very animal needs our help
F orests are disappearing
O ver our heads
R espect the trees
E verybody needs to help
S top deforestation
T o let animals live
A nimals lose their homes
T oo soon we won't have any animals left
I t kills animals
O ur forests are dying
N ever let us do this again.

Poppy Talbot (9)

Norton CE Primary School, Norton

Deforestation

D eforestation is bad

E very animal needs a home

F orests are dying

O rangutans do not have any bananas

R egrow the trees

E lephants are dying

S ave the trees

T rees are dying

A nimals need trees

T ry to help the Earth

I s this what we want...

O ne tree standing

N o trees standing.

Dennis Gilder (8)

Norton CE Primary School, Norton

Save Animals

A nimals die every day from plastic in the ocean

N othing is stopping us from helping the sea creatures

I n the ocean there are animals that are still waiting to be discovered

M ake us reuse plastic, it is a great idea

A nimals are amazing

L ots of animals are very special to me

S ave the animals! I'm not asking for a lot!

Grace Brooks (9)

Norton CE Primary School, Norton

Our Rainforests

R espect our rainforests

A nimals need our help

I nsects are getting stood on

N o trees should be cut down

F orests are disappearing

O ur planet needs our help

R ainforest animals will have no home

E very animal needs a home

S top cutting down trees

T rees grow taller than your heads.

Seren Loveridge (9)

Norton CE Primary School, Norton

The Baby Deer

The sun was setting
The deer was in the forest with his son
They were eating grass by the lake
A leopard jumped out of the forest and attacked
them
They ran into the majestic forest to get away
But the son was lost
The humans found him and took him somewhere
safe
When he grew older they released him back into
the wild
And he found his dad.

Ethan Pennington (8)
Norton CE Primary School, Norton

Worldwide Saving

R ecycling is important
E verything affects polar bears
C an help the climate
Y ou should help
C limate is affected
L ose your house, you decide
I n a way you will die
N ow think and stop
G o keep helping.

Owen Stancliffe (9)
Norton CE Primary School, Norton

Recycle

R ecycle what needs to be done
E arth needs your help
C an you fight for the world?
Y ou can't chop down trees
C an't you help?
L et's just fight the bad
E arth can't survive global warming.

Mia Barrett (8)
Norton CE Primary School, Norton

Save The Animals

A ll animals are dying

N o more trees cut down

I f we don't help we won't have the beauty

M ammals need our help

A ll hope is going down

L isten to your hearts

S ave the animals.

Luke Harris (9)
Norton CE Primary School, Norton

Do Not Kill Animals

T igers are in danger
I n the rainforests everything is dying
G ive tigers their homes back
E very animal is in danger
R ainforests are being chopped down
S top poachers killing tigers.

Austin Eastwood (8)
Norton CE Primary School, Norton

What Am I?

I am a sphere
People litter which makes me sad
Pollution is spreading in me
I grow trees, but people cut them down
What am I?

Answer: Planet Earth.

Seren Dorrington (9)

Norton CE Primary School, Norton

The Fun Forest

F un and games
O utdoors
R ainforest
E xplore
S ave the trees
T rees.

Jacob Cheeseman (8)
Norton CE Primary School, Norton

Environment

D on't litter on the beach, it's bad for the planet

O n the beach, if there's litter it would be good if you picked it up

N o one litter in the ocean, it's bad for the animals

T ell people that litter in the park is bad, if you see it pick it up

L ittering at your home is bad

I t's bad to litter, it can hurt animals and can hurt you

a T tempting to help other people is good and kind

T hrowing rubbish is really bad, it can hurt people

E verywhere I go I see rubbish

R unning you see rubbish, I want to see no rubbish.

Maliyah-Rae Brown (8)

Oak Field Primary School, Gibbonsdown

The Continents

There are seven continents in the world
When hurricanes twirl and twirl
Cutting down all the trees
Throwing litter in the seas
It's all bad, trees falling down
All the birds have a frown
Europe is one of the smallest
Asia is one of the biggest

Animals are going extinct
Don't waste any of your drink
All the litter in the sea
Fishes start to freak
Let's hope we can save the planet
Animals and nature, let's start saving it.

Alieu-leuan Bah (8)
Oak Field Primary School, Gibbonsdown

Earth

O ur Earth should be kept safe
U nder our Earth there are rocks
R euse instead of buying new things

E nvironment is very important to us
A nd we should keep it safe
R ecycling more stuff makes the environment better
T his is our planet, we need to keep it safe
H elp the environment be a nicer place to live.

Taya-May Jones (8)
Oak Field Primary School, Gibbonsdown

Please Pick Up Your Rubbish

Rubbish, rubbish, rubbish
A horrible thing for the environment
Rubbish, rubbish, rubbish
Please pick it up or the world may erupt

Rubbish, rubbish, rubbish
I see dirty beaches
Rubbish, rubbish, rubbish
And hear turtle screeches

Rubbish, rubbish, rubbish
More bins needed
Rubbish, rubbish, rubbish
So it's not left untreated.

Alfie Way (8)
Oak Field Primary School, Gibbonsdown

Trees

T rees are good, please don't cut them down
R eplant trees in green places
E very tree loses their leaves in autumn
E astern white pines are tall and thin
S ome birds lay eggs and build nests in trees

Please take care of our trees.

Theo Welch (8)
Oak Field Primary School, Gibbonsdown

Help The Bees

Be kind to the bees
Grow flowers to help them
Be kind to the bees
Put rubbish in the bin!
Be kind to the bees
Look after their hives
Be kind to the bees
Don't chop down trees!
Be kind to the bees
Please help them!

Rosanna Spragg (8)
Oak Field Primary School, Gibbonsdown

Don't Waste Water!

Don't run water when you're not using it
Dont leave water running
Don't leave the shower on
Or the taps in the kitchen
Don't leave the hose on
Don't pour water on the floor
Don't waste bottled water.

Brooklyn Bennett (9)
Oak Field Primary School, Gibbonsdown

Oceans

O ceans can be beautiful and blue
C lean beaches are needed
E verybody needs to bin rubbish
A nimals won't survive in dirty water
N ow we need to act to...
S ave our oceans!

Georgia Dudley (9)

Oak Field Primary School, Gibbonsdown

Saving Energy

E nergy bills are rising

N ever waste electricity

E verybody needs to help

R ecycle, reduce, reuse

G lobal warming ice is melting

Y es, we can save energy.

Lloyd Crump (8)

Oak Field Primary School, Gibbonsdown

Litter Pick

We need to help the planet
To get into a clean habit
Put rubbish in the bin
Otherwise there could be a ban
We need to help everyone
To show they care.

Romeo Hawker (9)
Oak Field Primary School, Gibbonsdown

Help The Animals

A haiku

Feed the animals
Be kind to the animals
Help the animals.

Melissa Rowlands (8)

Oak Field Primary School, Gibbonsdown

Rainforest

R ainforests are peaceful

A nd good to explore

I n rainforests you will see lots of animals

N ever go in the water near a current

F orests are full of adventures

O range monkeys are beautiful

R ivers we need to look after

E verybody needs to help

S ave the wildlife please

T he planet without nature and wildlife would be horrible.

Archie Walton (6)

Ralph Butterfield Primary School, Haxby

The Elements

T he world has earth, wind, water, fire, space
H ot could be in the desert
E arth can be found

E nter the water it is cold
L ive in the elements
E lements are good for you
M ild wind is in the sky
E lements can be dangerous
N ice elements can be everywhere
T he fire is an element
S pace too.

Finley Smith
Ralph Butterfield Primary School, Haxby

I Love Wildlife

W hales travel all around the world
I love wildlife!
L adybirds have spots and red skin
D id you know there is lots of nature around us?
L ots of hunters are coming out and finding animals
I love animals!
F riendly animals are amazing
E veryone needs to look after wildlife all the time.

Annabelle Smith (6)

Ralph Butterfield Primary School, Haxby

The Elements

T here are five elements
H ear the wind
E arth is amazing

E lements are amazing
L ook at the water
E lements help you
M ini fire turns big
E lements can help you
N o elements, no us
T he elements are helpful
S pace is awesome.

Jacob Humphrey (6)
Ralph Butterfield Primary School, Haxby

Rainforest

R ainforests have lots of animals

A nimals are adventurous

I t smells adventury in it

N ature is all around

F oxes are good

O ld trees are big

R oses are beautiful

E legant animals

S ee animals, big animals

T ender air, tender us.

Emma Gillah (6)

Ralph Butterfield Primary School, Haxby

Nature

N ature is beautiful with rainbows and colours in it.

A nimals need water so they can survive.

T all green leaves are changing colour in the rainforest.

U nique birds are nice.

R ainforests are good to explore.

E xploring rainforests is good to give me knowledge.

Lucy Kumar (6)

Ralph Butterfield Primary School, Haxby

What Am I?

I am a strong wish
You hear me in the night
Don't try and ignore me
I am your true light
You can see me but only in the night
All you can hear is a whisper
Everybody has me
But they are all different
I am imaginative
What am I?

Answer: A dream.

Maggie Gray (7)
Ralph Butterfield Primary School, Haxby

Nature

N ot many people realise how much nature there is.

A rainbow is a type of nature.

T oo hot then you might get a storm.

U nbelievable nature is what you should love.

R ubbish can really hurt animals.

E lements are important to have a wonderful world.

Annabel Cameron (7)
Ralph Butterfield Primary School, Haxby

Nature

N ature is a very wonderful thing!

A rainbow is in the sky above some beautiful pinky yellowy flowers

T he sky is a nice light clear blue colour

U nbeatable nature!

R ainbows are lots of pretty wonderful colours!

E vie, that's me, loves nature!

Evie Dickinson (7)
Ralph Butterfield Primary School, Haxby

Nature

N ature is good for your mental health

A rainbow brings joy because of the bright colours

T he swirling bright green grass

U nder the ground there are beautiful white rabbits

R abbits are calm in nature

E ggs are laid by fluffy chickens.

Maisie Gott (6)

Ralph Butterfield Primary School, Haxby

What Am I?

I have a sea the same colour as the sky
I have yellow sand
Seagulls fly around me
What am I?

Answer: The beach.

I have two sharp horns
I am dangerous
I live in Africa and Asia
What am I?

Answer: A rhino.

Kuba Madhavan (6)
Ralph Butterfield Primary School, Haxby

Forest

F orests are big and have wild animals
O ver the trees the birds fly
R ough trees grow
E xcited animals run, jump and climb on trees
S easons pass as the animals hibernate
T he forest trees break as the months pass.

Joe Thompson (6)
Ralph Butterfield Primary School, Haxby

Who Am I?

I am spiky
I am not often seen
I am a lovely plant
Who am I?

Answer: A nettle.

I am bumpy and rough
You might not see me
I am part of the chameleon family
Who am I?

Answer: A lizard.

Hazel Atherton (6)
Ralph Butterfield Primary School, Haxby

Who Am I?

I look like a poison berry with spots.
I am little just like a rock.
I have tiny legs.
People like to hold me.
You can see my age if I have spots.
I only come out in the day.
Who am I?

Answer: A ladybird.

Ruby Walton (6)
Ralph Butterfield Primary School, Haxby

What Am I?

Lots of trees live here.
Lots of animals live here.
Lots of plants live here and you can get water here too.
There is lots of mud on the floor.
There are ponds here.
What am I?

Answer: A jungle.

Thomas Elsom (7)
Ralph Butterfield Primary School, Haxby

Arctic

    A rctic ice is melting
w **R** ecking animals' homes
    C learing polar bears' food
    T aking polar bears' lives
    I ce melts beneath
    C racking ice drops polar bears.

Thomas Crundwell (7)

Ralph Butterfield Primary School, Haxby

Nature

N ature shows beauty.

A nimals need to be respected.

T all trees sway in the wind.

U nder the deep blue sea.

R espect the animals!

E verything needs to be respected.

Sophia Dodsworth (6)

Ralph Butterfield Primary School, Haxby

Who Am I?

I am found anywhere
I am home to everyone
It's easy for people to destroy me
I am a planet
Lots of people and animals live on me.
Who am I?

Answer: I am the Earth.

Jay Madhavan (6)
Ralph Butterfield Primary School, Haxby

Forest

F orests are important
O ver time they grow
R ocks are black all around
E xplore more
S ilent as you walk
T o hear the birds sing.

Oliver Ryan (6)
Ralph Butterfield Primary School, Haxby

Nature

N ature is all around us

A nimals are waking up

T all trees with green leaves

U nder the blue sky

R ainbows

E veryone help nature.

Amy Saidykhan (6)

Ralph Butterfield Primary School, Haxby

Who Am I?

I am the lazy one in my family
I hunt at night
When I hunt at night I hunt in a team
I am a carnivore
I live in a cave
Who am I?

Answer: A lion.

Autumn Bodden (6)

Ralph Butterfield Primary School, Haxby

What Am I?

I am sometimes cold.
I am in the sky.
You can't see me.
Birds fly in me.
I'm normally in the cold seasons.
What am I?

Answer: The wind.

Noah Thorpe (7)
Ralph Butterfield Primary School, Haxby

What Am I?

I grow on trees and bushes
I change colour in the seasons
I come in different shapes and sizes
Insects live on me
What am I?

Answer: Leaves.

Emily Frank (7)

Ralph Butterfield Primary School, Haxby

Who Am I?

I sleep on your bed
I am furry
I can be ginger and black
I have 4 legs
I have a short tail
I am small
Who am I?

Answer: A cat.

Chester Bell (6)

Ralph Butterfield Primary School, Haxby

Who Am I?

I am a mammal.
I live in a deep, dark ocean.
I am really heavy.
I am endangered.
I am a carnivore.
Who am I?

Answer: A blue whale.

Vinnie Varley (6)
Ralph Butterfield Primary School, Haxby

Who Am I?

I have hard skin
I am deadly
I have sharp teeth
I am sneaky
Sometimes I don't mind humans
Who am I?

Answer: A Komodo dragon.

Tess Holliday (6)
Ralph Butterfield Primary School, Haxby

Who Am I?

I have a pink tail
I eat cheese
I squeak
I have white fur
My tail has stripes on
I am little
Who am I?

Answer: A mouse.

William Greaves (6)
Ralph Butterfield Primary School, Haxby

Who Am I?

I have sharp teeth
I have a long tail on my bum
I have three claws
I have three toes
Who am I?

Answer: I'm an Indominus rex!

Noah Wardell (5)
Ralph Butterfield Primary School, Haxby

Who Am I?

I have wings
I have sharp teeth
I have a tail
I have a very strong body
I have powerful legs
Who am I?

Answer: A dragon.

Alfie Ward (5)
Ralph Butterfield Primary School, Haxby

Who Am I?

I live in the trees up high
I live in a hot place
I am in danger
I can cause injuries all the time
Who am I?

Answer: A koala.

Olivia Strange (6)
Ralph Butterfield Primary School, Haxby

Who Am I?

I have a grey furry body
I live in Australia
I am cute like a bunny
I have a black and shiny nose
Who am I?

Answer: A koala.

Martha Arbon (5)
Ralph Butterfield Primary School, Haxby

What Am I?

I am in the sky at night
There are lots of me
I am yellow
I am in the sky with the moon
What am I?

Answer: The stars.

Freya Boothman (7)
Ralph Butterfield Primary School, Haxby

Who Am I?

I can fly
I can copy what people say
My wings go up and down
I am blue, yellow and red
Who am I?

Answer: A parrot.

Kyrah Amaral (6)
Ralph Butterfield Primary School, Haxby

YoungWriters® Est. 1991

Wildlife

Who am I?
My size is big
My colour is grey
My children splash in the water
Who am I?

Answer: I am an elephant.

Molly Thrower (7)
Ralph Butterfield Primary School, Haxby

What Am I?

I am sparkly and pointy
I am yellow
I shine and I glow
There are lots of me
What am I?

Answer: I am a star.

Lucas Newton-Bacon (7)
Ralph Butterfield Primary School, Haxby

Who Am I?

I am colourful
You find me in the rainforest
I make noise
I fly in the sky
Who am I?

Answer: A parrot.

Martha Clark (7)
Ralph Butterfield Primary School, Haxby

What Am I?

I am painful!
I was large in 1666
I am yellow, orange and red when you draw me
What am I?

Answer: Fire.

Max Snow (7)
Ralph Butterfield Primary School, Haxby

Who Am I?

I live on snowy mountains
I have spots all over me
I am so soft
Who am I?

Answer: I am a snow leopard.

Esmée Wilkins Raw (6)
Ralph Butterfield Primary School, Haxby

Who Am I?

I live in Australia
Nearly at the bottom of the sea
I have a sad face
Who am I?

Answer: A blobfish.

Millie Macfarlane (6)
Ralph Butterfield Primary School, Haxby

Who Am I?

I am blue
I am a sea monster
I have red eyes
I have tentacles
Who am I?

Answer: *The Kraken.*

Jack Evans (7)
Ralph Butterfield Primary School, Haxby

What Am I?

I am used to drink
I can be recycled
I can be squished easily
What am I?

A plastic bottle.

Esmae Read (6)

Ralph Butterfield Primary School, Haxby

Who Am I?

I live in the sea
I eat fish
I have fins
I have a tail
Who am I?

Answer: A dolphin.

Jacob Wright (6)
Ralph Butterfield Primary School, Haxby

Who Am I?

I am red
I live in the trees
I eat bananas
Who am I?

Answer: I am a monkey.

Harry Sturdy-Evans (5)
Ralph Butterfield Primary School, Haxby

Who Am I?

I have wings
I live in a tree
I fly every day
Who am I?

Answer: A bird.

Scarlett Turner (6)
Ralph Butterfield Primary School, Haxby

Who Am I?

I have orange fur
I have furry ears
Who am I?

Answer: I am a fox.

Emily Elsom (5)
Ralph Butterfield Primary School, Haxby

Our Planet

The Earth's lungs are a beautiful place,
The trees, the air, everything is its trace,
Animals live throughout the forest,
Earthworms live in the soil,
Monkeys hang in the canopy trees,
But what if I told you something more dark?
Something that made you want to play your part?
Trees chopped down for palm oil we 'so need',
It's not that important,
But have you ever thought, *what about the trees?*
We draw on things we need,
CO_2 isn't as bad with our trees.
What about the trees?
Orangutans, sloths and even parakeets are losing
their homes, because let me tell you,
Nobody has stopped to take a quick minute and
think:
What about the trees?
What about these actions too?
What is the Earth with this attitude?
What about the trees?

Rhea Butwell (10)

Richard Whittington Primary School, Bishop's Stortford

Our Planet

We need to think fast and think about the animals
Helpless turtles being strangled to death
It makes you think, think about all the plastic we
need to recycle.

How can we not see what we're doing?
Only you can make a difference, only you can
change it
Everyone can make a difference.

Let the animals thrive in their habitats,
Now come on, we need to think fast and act fast
Hopes and dreams are dying, animals are
becoming extinct.

Now come on, we need to make a difference
together.

Noah Groom (10)
Richard Whittington Primary School, Bishop's Stortford

Our Planet

Deforestation, it's across our nation.
Animals are endangered, some are extinct.
Not all stuff is renewable but some can save our planet.
Just recycle, it will help.
Saving the wildlife is saving little girls' and boys' dreams around the world.
There is no Planet B, so stop hunting animals, stop cutting down the trees.
Save our planet before there is no more planet left to live on.
Deforestation, it's all across our nation.

There is no Planet B!

Paige Gamble (10)
Richard Whittington Primary School, Bishop's Stortford

Helping The Forest

Trees are being cut down by people.
Trees are full of energy by providing air to us.
There aren't as many trees in the world because...
Trees are being set on fire by climate change.

Our planet has more water than trees.
Trees are really important when it comes to
providing air
Because if there aren't any more trees, humans
won't be able to survive.
So help our planet now before it's too late.
People can grow food from trees.

Teodor Bosca (10)
Richard Whittington Primary School, Bishop's Stortford

Our Planet

Species are close to becoming extinct.
Antarctica is melting and polar bears are falling.
Our fishy friends are dying.
A certain amount of animals are in this world.
Why don't we become a team and protect animals from their deaths?
Why don't we save our world?
So think about all the endangered animals and ice melting.
Get off your laptops and save the planet.
Do you want to save our planet.
Save our animals and their habitats?

Maisie Hicking (10)
Richard Whittington Primary School, Bishop's Stortford

Our Planet

Icebergs are melting,
We need to play our part,
Summer is coming,
When climate change really starts.

Before the Earth crashes and burns,
From methane and toxic cow f****,
We need to make the tables turn,
When climate change really starts.

If you want a better future,
Maybe we'll keep some cars,
Just listen to what I will teach ya,
When climate change really starts.

Emily Beaufond (10)
Richard Whittington Primary School, Bishop's Stortford

Our Planet

Climate change is caused by human activity
Deforestation is killing wildlife, releasing
greenhouse gases
Warming up the planet for the cattle and palm oil

Oceans are filling up with plastic, it's hurting
marine life
Whales and sharks are harpooned for money
Tsunamis are coming too often
A sign of danger.

But there's a chance...

Will Bennett
Richard Whittington Primary School, Bishop's Stortford

Our Planet

Plastic swims through me, making me cry,
My fish, my fish, soon they will die.

Deforestation is not what I need,
Civilisation, and now I'm a reed.

Cooking with palm oil,
Whilst we fight against foil.

But here comes something better,
Like the reign of Greta...

The Big Green Poetry Machine!

Andrew Randle (10)
Richard Whittington Primary School, Bishop's Stortford

Our Planet

There is so much drama
And people getting bad karma
There's no harmony
And people invading government property
There's so many people dying
Don't hear other people crying
People are killing
And they don't even listen to the sirens ringing
They ring 999
But they put them on hold a thousand times.

Kai Lumley (10)

Richard Whittington Primary School, Bishop's Stortford

Our Planet

Save our planet
Clean our oceans
Our world needs our help
No more polluting
Keep our oceans clear
Animals can't survive in our mess
Let our animals swim in the clean oceans.

O ur planet
C lean our oceans
E nvironment
A nimals need help
N ow ocean clean-up.

Harlie Stewart (10)

Richard Whittington Primary School, Bishop's Stortford

Our Planet

We may have land but what about the water?
Having plastic thrown in it all the time
Hurting its species like fish and turtles
Maybe you can hear their crying as they're dying
But what about the other side?
It's coral and soft sand
It may not all be good but it is still beautiful.

Ottilai Jermy (10)

Richard Whittington Primary School, Bishop's Stortford

Our Planet

P lanet Earth needs us now

R evive our planet

O ur cruelty needs to stop

T oday one plastic bottle can change

E veryone is included

C an you help me from now on?

T he planet needs our help by recycling our rubbish.

Lily Springate (10)

Richard Whittington Primary School, Bishop's Stortford

Our Planet

Our world is dying
They're not surviving
We don't care but we should
Cutting down trees is not good
That's why we are dying not surviving
Recycling is good
Throwing away is bad
Killing turtles and jellyfish
Always care for the world.

Sonnie Lynch (10)
Richard Whittington Primary School, Bishop's Stortford

Our Planet

O ur fishy folk are dying

C aps get stuck in turtles' throats

E ndangered, whales' stomachs are taken hostage

A ll birds are eating toxins

N ow stop and listen! Can you hear the animals crying for help?

Kieran Dedman (10)

Richard Whittington Primary School, Bishop's Stortford

Our Planet

O n the coast people drop plastic

C ausing me to be polluted

E very day it gets more drastic

A fter a while I'll make lots of tsunamis

N ow help me friend, or I'll never be seen again.

Sam Jones (10)

Richard Whittington Primary School, Bishop's Stortford

Our Planet

P rotect our wildlife
L earn what's best for the environment
A nimals are becoming endangered
N o more pollution
E arth could use your help
T ell others to help our planet.

Elly-May Robertson (10)
Richard Whittington Primary School, Bishop's Stortford

Our Planet

We can't run,
We can't hide,
Now it's time for you to decide,
There is pollution everywhere,
In the sea and in the air,
Us animals, we are living too,
So think,
Is this planet just for you?

Aaya El-Sharkawy (10)

Richard Whittington Primary School, Bishop's Stortford

Our Planet

H elp the homes of animals

A ction must begin

B ears are not surviving

I nclude other people

T ell others, spread the word

A nimals are dying

T ime is running out.

Aleksandra Dopcheva (10)
Richard Whittington Primary School, Bishop's Stortford

Our Planet

Deforestation causes a commotion
Animals are dying
Animals are crying
Chimpanzees are falling from the trees
Deforestation is not for me.

Ryan Thomson (10)
Richard Whittington Primary School, Bishop's Stortford

Help The Nature

H elping nature saves the animals
E ven when we are sad nature brings us up
L eaving nature to burn would be bad for wildlife
P eople should keep nature safe

T he nature has saved us food
H igh up or low down, we see nature
E ven though we eat it it helps us grow

N ature is the best, we like it, it likes us
A nd nature is our best friend
T he animals might be creepy but they are living
U nder us is nature everywhere
R eading a book by yourself outside is good
E verything we see is nature and we belong with it.

Lucas Rogers (10)

St John's CE Primary Academy, Stafford

YoungWriters®
Est. 1991

Save The Polar Bear!

P olar bears are in danger
O h and poor polar bears live on the ice
L ots of polar bears have to keep children on the ice
A nd polar bears' ice is breaking
R eally polar bears cannot swim a lot

B ecause lots of polar bears are out on the ice
E arth is really like their homes
A nimals have got to live here
R emember polar bears live with us
S ave the polar bears, they need your help.

Ellie Booth (9)
St John's CE Primary Academy, Stafford

The Environment

E nergy produced by harming the planet.
N ature in danger, we need to save it!
V iolent storms attack our Earth.
I t needs to stop now!
R ainforests getting cut for wood.
O r getting destroyed for land to use.
N ature is getting blasted away.
M etals buildings rise through the ground
E nding all the wildlife around.
N ot the way our planet should be.
T he world needs us, so save it!

Devansh Pun (9)
St John's CE Primary Academy, Stafford

Sea Animals

S ea animals are dying from plastic

E very sea animal is hurt by plastic

A s sea animals are dying people are throwing more plastic in the sea

A nimals have not done anything to you

N ever hit them

I s it necessary to shoot them and eat them?

M e and you like animals

A re animals mean to you and me?

L ike animals instead of hurting them

S o help animals instead of leaving them to die.

Thomas Wright (10)
St John's CE Primary Academy, Stafford

Polar Bears (Save Our Planet)

P olar bears are great animals, living
O n tiny icebergs that are getting
L ittler and littler until they're gone
A nd the bears are losing
R eally big pieces of land and are going

B e kinder to our planet
E arth is getting weaker
A nd we are killing it, we
R eally need to stop throwing plastic in the ocean
S o the polar bears need your help.

Ethan Harley (10)
St John's CE Primary Academy, Stafford

The Polar Bears

P olar bears so cute and fluffy
O n the ice playing with their friends
L ooking for some yummy food to eat
A ll the ice is slowly melting
R eally sad that all of their homes are
  disappearing

B e respectful to our planet
E arth is getting more hurt
A nimals are getting hurt every day
R espect the sea and everywhere
S ave all the polar bears!

Bella Langford (9)
St John's CE Primary Academy, Stafford

Endangered

E very animal should be safe

N ever getting hurt

D anger is everywhere, even in space

A nimals are so cute, even in the dirt

N ot to stop and help them is just rude

G etting them hurt means you have an attitude

E ven if they don't look good

R ainforests are their homes

E nvironment needs to be good

D anger lurks in the woods.

Phoebe Bull (10)
St John's CE Primary Academy, Stafford

A True Wish

In the night I fell asleep
I woke up in a new world
My wish... huge trees, frogs leaping
Especially no plastic
But then the clock rang
I woke up to the reality of small trees and birds
hurt
No frogs were leaping
I walked to a 'plastic' pond
I know dreams can't always come true
But the thing I know best
Is that everyone can change that
I know they could come true...

Leah Sinclair (10)
St John's CE Primary Academy, Stafford

Nature's Riddles

I am a place
I don't get that much rain for a long time
I am very dry
I have cracks
What am I?

I am a thick forest
I have tropical places
I get a lot of rain
I have many creatures
What am I?

I have seeds inside me
I have a lot of petals
It would be impossible for me without water or
sunlight
I am colourful
What am I?

Marvin Limbu (9)
St John's CE Primary Academy, Stafford

Wildlife

W hy do you cut down trees?
I n the wild animals are dying
L ove the Earth and keep it safe
D anger is not good for our animals
L ife would be boring without the wild
I love the wild, but it is going
F ire and flame spread through the forest
E nvironment is falling apart slowly.

Alona Shinu (10)

St John's CE Primary Academy, Stafford

Recycle All

R ecycle
E ndangered animals need help
N ever stop recycling
E very tree is living
W e have to protect nature
A lways protect the environment
B e kind to the environment
L ove nature
E veryone needs trees.

Sarah Wright (10)
St John's CE Primary Academy, Stafford

YoungWriters®
Est. 1991

What Am I?

There is always something in the air
The Earth can be endangered
I can damage the environment
I am everywhere in the skies
I can be toxic to the planet
I am a waste or poison
What am I?

Answer: Pollution.

Anusha Gurung (9)
St John's CE Primary Academy, Stafford

Nature

N ever pollute
A ct kind to our planet
T rees don't deserve to be cut down
U ndo the mistakes you've made to our planet
R espect our planet
E nvironments are dying.

Ernie Kenderdine (10)

St John's CE Primary Academy, Stafford

Help The Planet With Your Friend

Stop using diesel and switch to electric
If you don't have the money get a bike
Don't forget a helmet with a good trick
Some good shoes are Nike
When I got a bike
I rode with my friend Mike.

Thomas Devine (10)
St John's CE Primary Academy, Stafford

Save Our Planet

I love oceans, they are good for you,
You agree, do you?
So join the crew
Don't chop trees or plants, we need them to survive
So we don't die
I'm just full of pride.

Charlie Grantham (10)
St John's CE Primary Academy, Stafford

Planet Riddle

I'm round
You live on me
I'm the third closest to the sun
I've got one moon
God made me
I'm beautiful
Who am I?

Answer: The Earth.

Arthur Sutton (9)
St John's CE Primary Academy, Stafford

Save The Forests And Jungles

Save our jungles,
Animals live there,
I'm almost extinct, so help us too,
Pick up your litter,
Do you not know what you do?
So pick up your litter,
Please don't leave it.
Waterfalls and rivers flow down,
I love the jungle so please don't waste it,
Save it!
The forest is dying, I don't know what to do,
Please help me and the forest too.
Wherever I look, trees are chopped down,
Help me save the forest and the forest will help you.
Animals live in the forest and jungle,
They need your help so help them too.
Now stand together and help us, they help you.
If you want a nice place to live,
Help me and the forests too.

Annabel John (9)
Wix & Wrabness Primary School, Wix

Concrete Jungle

Dear future Earth
We would like to make an apology
An apology to put green on this planet
Not grey, black or any of those colours

Dear future Earth
We promise to fix this
We like green and trees
Not replacing it with concrete

Dear future Earth
We want to see green leaves on the grass
We don't want to see plants die

Dear future Earth
We want to see trees standing up
Not the trees in half and replaced with a house

Dear future Earth
We will put the green on the trees
On the ground and feel the peace

Dear future Earth
We can see the mountains
But we will find stone on them
And replace the stones with leaves.

Leon Fulljames (9)
Wix & Wrabness Primary School, Wix

Nature's Heart

We all have a heart and you're chopping me down
Too many times for us to put it down on charts
Leave the trees alone please
Who do you think has put in an effort
To save a healthy heart?
We are pieces of art
We are pieces of art and you're crushing me like a
jam tart
I work hard, produce for you healthy air
I could've lived on
But you're giving me death and humiliation early
It's such a painful thing to think about
The pain you've left me in
You're destroying homes and leaving the blame
For doing these ridiculous things
All just for money
This is a big mistake
Leave the trees alone, please.

Felicity Randall (10)

Wix & Wrabness Primary School, Wix

Nature I Know You

Flowers are purple
Grass is green
Weeds are now never seen
Sun so bright, night so dark
All the animals go to the park
Flowers yellow, white and blue
The wind is howling right at you
Trees grow over the grass
My world is the one that lasts
Grass growing, people talking
Rain pouring and animals hunting
That's my dream world
I know I'm little but listen to my words
I know I'm not the only passionate girl in the world
Please help the world with me.

Anise Arthey (9)
Wix & Wrabness Primary School, Wix

My Precious Park

My precious park is perfect,
Some flowers are blooming, some aren't,
Plants need food to get bigger, some don't.

Stop building houses on me,
I am not very strong,
Help me bulldoze them down,
I can taste grass and other stuff.

You have to go through the task of dog poo,
The most putrid, unbreathable thing,
You can hear dogs, cars and many other things.

You can smell wet grass and other stuff,
You can feel grass, metalwork and sunlight.

Thomas Mackintosh (8)

Wix & Wrabness Primary School, Wix

My Wildlife

I can see sealions roaring and swimming
Crabs hitting stones and pinching people
Lions roaring and hunting animals
I can hear orangutans crying because people are
chopping down their homes
Grass swishing around
Mice squeaking
Ponies having a race
Mandrills arguing the whole entire day
Spider monkeys playing football
Gorillas lifting weights
Frogs acting like Superman
Chimps having a relaxing day
Ladybugs flying like planes.

Mason Hicks (9)

Wix & Wrabness Primary School, Wix

World Of Nature

A forest of green is the best you've ever seen
Please don't be mean to the environment
Love nature, look after nature, never disrespect
nature
This is for the trees being cut down
And all of the animals being killed just for food
This is the world of nature
Harmless birds sitting in their nests
The next thing they know, they're shot
Stop shooting birds or any creatures
Because it's cruel
This is my world of nature.

Madison Kindred (10)
Wix & Wrabness Primary School, Wix

My Private Beach

Treat me well because I am here to let you play on
me
I have feelings too
I am not here for you to be mean to me
I don't like rubbish
Glass hurts me
Don't put rubbish on me because it's bad for the
environment
Recycle your rubbish
Let me live peacefully
Respect me
I respect you
You should never ever be mean to the Earth
No one likes a rubbish-y beach
Everyone likes a nice, clean, peaceful beach.

Dolly Demi Lucas Angus (9)
Wix & Wrabness Primary School, Wix

This Is My World

I am Mother Earth, this is my world
I do not like you because this is my world
All you do is take over my fields
Shoot my birds for fun
And chop down my trees
You are not allowed to do that
Because this is my world

It was calm and peaceful before humans polluted my air
Don't you listen, stop throwing your rubbish out your windows
My grass is dying because of you
Just stop, this is my world.

Erin Philipson (9)
Wix & Wrabness Primary School, Wix

This Is For The Earth

This is for the Earth that we are destroying
This is for the trees who give us oxygen
This is for the animals that give us meat
We are destroying the ground that we live and
walk on
Put more rubbish in the bin before it's too late
This place used to be a rainforest but now it's like
a desert
Stop throwing rubbish in the sea or on the ground
Stop cutting trees down
This is for our Earth.

Rueben Smith (10)
Wix & Wrabness Primary School, Wix

My Forest

Wind blowing in the sky,
Glistening grass on the shining floor,
Light green leaves falling,
Spraying trees through the wind.

Please stop cutting me down, it really hurts,
Leaves waving,
Birds tweeting, squirrels leaping,
Air blowing, people talking.

Stop throwing rubbish in my home,
Creatures crawling,
Birds singing,
Leaping frogs, crouching bugs.

Jacob Boswell (7)
Wix & Wrabness Primary School, Wix

Please Listen

Pick up litter, don't be bitter
I know I am a child but please listen
The trees and the sea are being polluted and cut
down
Stop making animals' homes burnt to the ground
Mother Nature is in a great state at this moment
in time
I know I am a child but please listen
Please try to recycle
Stop burning the jungle and turning away
I know I am a child but please listen.

Laney Gansbuhler (10)
Wix & Wrabness Primary School, Wix

Save The Planet Today!

Save the planet
Save the trees
Save the polar bears
Stop climate change
Protect wildlife
Stop pollution
Save nature
Stop wildfires
Rainforests are burning
Save the Earth from global warming
You can save the Earth today
Stop smoking
Stop the greenhouse gases
It's bad for the environment
Stop wasting electricity
Help our planet today!

Sammy Fenton (8)
Wix & Wrabness Primary School, Wix

Wildlife

Foxes howling,
Deer prowling,
Birds singing,
Fishes swimming,
Rabbits eating,
Mice squeaking,
Grasshoppers hopping,
Butterflies flying,
Dolphins leaping,
Cows mooing,
Bears sleeping,
Lions roaring,
Elephants trumpeting,
Monkeys ooh ooh aahing,
Crocodiles snapping,
Bees buzzing,
Sheep baaing,
Chickens clucking.

Thomas Thornicroft (8)

Wix & Wrabness Primary School, Wix

My Forest

Don't chop me down
Don't turn me into sofas, chairs and stairs
Remember, I help you breathe

Feel my bark and soft leaves
Don't bring your white shirt
I've got staining grass

Listen to my music boxes singing in the trees
Look at my perfect logs
Pick my berries and mushrooms too
There's always something new to do.

Phoenix Hasson (9)
Wix & Wrabness Primary School, Wix

My Lovely Park

I love my park,
But sometimes I feel put off,
When I see rubbish and dog poo on the floor,
I feel sad when I hear it say, "Stop throwing
rubbish on my face,"
I see cigarette tops and broken glass,
I hear screaming babies,
Squabbling teenagers as well,
I taste some snacks,
That cheers me up,
Then I go off again playing my game.

Finn Muldoon (8)
Wix & Wrabness Primary School, Wix

YoungWriters
Est. 1991

My Meadow

Stop chucking rubbish in my home,
You're killing my friends and family,
You're hurting us.

You're hurting my feet when I step on glass,
You're hurting my feelings,
Do you know that?

The cockerel is an alarm clock,
The chickens are clucking,
Pigs are eating, sheep pooing,
Goats moaning.

Neve Poppy Cansdale (8)
Wix & Wrabness Primary School, Wix

The Sea

A wavy blue heaven
The spot of desires
But now she keeps getting higher
Fossil fuel burning
And we are still not learning
That all of our actions are wrong
Icebergs melt, there is no doubt
There's really no way of flushing it out
The sea needs something new
The future really starts with you.

Holly Vincent (9)
Wix & Wrabness Primary School, Wix

My Park

Birds tweeting in the sky,
Roots lying on the ground,
Vines lying on the leaves,
Vines hugging all the trees,
Luscious grass,
Squealing children,
Avoiding glass,
Blooming flowers,
Hiding trees,
Birds tweeting in the breeze,
Birds sitting on rocks,
Little legs on docks.

Robert Kindred (8)
Wix & Wrabness Primary School, Wix

My Forest

Trees are swaying grass,
Glistening plastic rustling,
Blooming flowers in the breeze,
Birds tweeting like a radio,
Stop cutting me down!
It hurts!
Stop picking me,
I'm growing slowly,
Long vines hugging trees,
Calming music, trees swaying,
Leaves moving.

Lydia Thornton (9)
Wix & Wrabness Primary School, Wix

YoungWriters® Est. 1991

Save Our World

Flowers are blue, leaves are green
This is my world
Wind howling, leaves falling
Trees breathing
This is my world
Grass growing, gardeners gardening
Birds singing
This is my world
Rain pouring, sun so bright
All my feelings come at night
This is my world.

Freya Good (9)
Wix & Wrabness Primary School, Wix

My Shiny Beach

At my beach, fishes leap,
Up and down, around the ground.
Stones and bones going down,
The boiling sand around my hand.
Pick up litter, my picture, bright or light
It's in my sight.
Birds are tweeting in a meeting,
All day long as they sing their song.

Thomas Burls (8)
Wix & Wrabness Primary School, Wix

YoungWriters Est. 1991

Our Animals

O utdoors,
U nder the stars,
R elying on us.

A nimals,
N ative,
I n need of care,
M ore love for animals,
A ll shapes and sizes,
L ove and kindness,
S ave the animals.

Harry Spence (9)
Wix & Wrabness Primary School, Wix

My Forest

Diamond flowers in the breeze,
Creeping vines hugging trees,
Deer prowling around,
Crickets jumping from leaf to leaf,
Stop cutting me down, it hurts!
Tweeting birds like a radio,
Lovely lakes and glistening grass,
Cheetahs with little legs.

Finley Bartlett (9)
Wix & Wrabness Primary School, Wix

My Playground

Swaying trees,
Green grass,
Long streets,
No need for glass.

Stop chopping down the trees,
It will ruin all the breeze,
They provide oxygen, you know,
So let me grow.

No one likes litter,
It's all very bitter,
That's why it's better,
To bin your litter.

Oliver Walmsley (9)
Wix & Wrabness Primary School, Wix

Save Us!

Stop cutting me down
Stop throwing rubbish in our home
You're hurting my heart
And my feelings
Stop throwing glass on the floor
You're hurting my feet
So please stop
Because we don't like it!

Millie Robb (7)
Wix & Wrabness Primary School, Wix

The Forest

Stop throwing plastic at my feet
You're cutting me down
You're hurting me
I care and help you, so can you help me too?
I am green, I am pretty when I'm clean,
I'm dirty and I don't feel well.

Evana Hughes (8)

Wix & Wrabness Primary School, Wix

Woodlice

W andering around
O ak tree climber
O ver the logs
D anger everywhere
L izard crawling near
I nching closer
C rawling over
E ver so scared.

Mason Bartlett (7)
Wix & Wrabness Primary School, Wix

Secret Garden

My garden is not a garden,
It's a secret garden,
Trees talk,
People use chalk,
Daisies grow above the maze,
The squirrels zoom,
The insects dance,
The children play,
People say,
This is a secret garden.

Mason Walmsley (7)
Wix & Wrabness Primary School, Wix

Forest

The forest is a peaceful and beautiful place
Where animals come to a lake
To drink and where they are safe
Sometimes danger all around
Chopped down trees
Stop! It hurts me you know.

Adam Lee (7)
Wix & Wrabness Primary School, Wix

The Forest

Please stop cutting me and my friends and family down
I give you oxygen to breathe and live
I can grow apples for you to eat and pears and plums
In my leaves are birds living.

Erin Barker (8)

Wix & Wrabness Primary School, Wix

My Garden

M ajestic,
Y awning,

G leaming sun,
A nimals,
R abbits and roses,
D affodils,
E xcited,
N aughty.

Billy Spence (7)
Wix & Wrabness Primary School, Wix

Pollution

Pollution is bad for the environment
Because it kills the animals in the water
Leave the Earth alone
Why are we throwing rubbish in the water?
There are bins around.

Ryan Smith (9)
Wix & Wrabness Primary School, Wix

My Favourite Woods

Wrabness Woods is full of trees
Water in the woods
Full of trees rustling
Bugs and butterflies and insects
Save the animals
You are killing their home!

Coen Smith (7)
Wix & Wrabness Primary School, Wix

My Forest

F licking flies
O aks standing proud
R oaming foxes
E mpty nests
S quirrels like gymnasts
T rees are life!

Romeo Thursting (7)

Wix & Wrabness Primary School, Wix

Rivers

R ough and calm water
I n and out fishes
V ery cool leap
E very picture speaks
R eally precious.

Jake Grimwood-Murray (7)
Wix & Wrabness Primary School, Wix

Beach

B reaking waves

E veryone swimming

A ll the litter

C rabs crawling

H elp keep me clean.

Ellie Oldroyd (7)

Wix & Wrabness Primary School, Wix

The Beach

B reaking waves,
E verybody swimming,
A fter,
C lean the beach,
H elp it stay nice.

Harrison Houlton (8)
Wix & Wrabness Primary School, Wix

The Park

P eaceful heaven
A ll children happy
R otting food
K eep me safe and clean.

Dylan Thorndike (7)
Wix & Wrabness Primary School, Wix

Parks

P laying
A nimals and children
R unning
K eep me nice and clean.

Rocco Smith (7)
Wix & Wrabness Primary School, Wix

There's No Planet B

There's no Planet B,
So what should we do?
Let's take a look with me and you!

Stop polluting the sea,
It's bad for the fish,
The plastic goes in,
Against their wish.

There's no Planet B,
So what should we do?
Let's take a look with me and you!

Stop polluting the air,
It's causing some coughs,
It's bad for asthma,
Don't care, you all scoff.

There's no Planet B,
So what should we do?
Let's take a look with me and you!

Stop killing the animals,
Just for cash,
You'll make them extinct,
Stop being rash!

There's no Planet B,
So what should we do?
Let's take a look with me and you!

Do the 3 Rs,
It's not that tough,
My pen is made
Of recycled stuff!

There's no Planet B,
So what should we do?
Let's take a look with me and you!

So now you see why
We care so much,
Save the planet,
With a helpful touch.

Megan Wickins (11)
Woodbury Salterton CE Primary, Woodbury Salterton

Lumberjacks And Deforestation

L umberjacks destroy our only world!

U nderneath, the roots are dying.

M others keep their children safe.

B e the mother of trees.

E ven if they keep on chopping, save wildlife.

R ebuild trees and wildlife.

J ust stop it now!

A xes, get rid of axes!

C lever people wouldn't want to hurt wildlife.

K ick lumberjacks into space!

S ave the wildlife.

Ivy Regan (8)

Woodbury Salterton CE Primary, Woodbury Salterton

Soft Plastics

Stop throwing rubbish,
Stop recycling soft plastics,
This is so disastrous,
So stop this now.

Ocean life is hard now,
Because we ruined their home,
So we should fix this,
And stop recycling soft plastics now.

Now we should try our best,
To make their home better again,
We can do it,
Just act now.

Please help,
Please rescue,
Just stop and think,
Or just believe.

Luca Ficken (10)
Woodbury Salterton CE Primary, Woodbury Salterton

Stop Littering

Stop littering
Stop littering, be a...

S uper eco-hero
T errific world changer
O ptimistic ocean saver
P lastic picker

L ife changer
I nspirational
T urtle saver
T errific world saver
E xtinction preventer
R euse, reduce, recycler
I mpactful animal saver
N ature lover
G reta Thunberg follower.

Tessa Wickins (9)
Woodbury Salterton CE Primary, Woodbury Salterton

Protect Our Planet

We live in a wonderful place,
On our planet Earth,
Where there's not just a human race,
But now it's getting hurt!

There is no Planet B,
So why are you poaching?
Why are you littering the sea?
There is no reason for boasting!

Governments can talk all they like,
But actions mean more than words,
So save the tiger, snake and pike,
And save our planet Earth.

Olivia Drake (10)
Woodbury Salterton CE Primary, Woodbury Salterton

Woodbury Salterton Weather

The weather in my village,
Can sometimes be extreme,
From 32 degrees in summer,
To -4 and freezing!

My mum planted daffodil bulbs,
They come back every year,
And when I see the green stems,
I know spring is finally here.

I prefer my garden when it's hot,
I play in it a lot,
Water fights and trampolines,
The fun times never stop.

Brodie Nosworthy (11)
Woodbury Salterton CE Primary, Woodbury Salterton

My Two Pet Rats

M y rats are the best thing in the world
wh **Y** are they so cute?

P et rats, you could buy them
E very day they get cuter
T he best rats in the world

R ats are so cute
A rlo and Arbie, that's their names
T he male rats sometimes fight each other
S ometimes they go on mute.

Skyla Melluish (10)

Woodbury Salterton CE Primary, Woodbury Salterton

Climate Change

C limate change is caused by cars and pollution
L ots of ice is melting because of climate change
I think climate change is bad
M illions of cars are polluting the planet
A nimals are in danger because of climate change
T he ice is melting
E verybody needs to stop climate change.

Florence Robinson (8)

Woodbury Salterton CE Primary, Woodbury Salterton

Deforestation

What is it about?
People chopping down trees, right?
Yes, well done you!

Why do they do it?
To get food for themselves
What's the point of that?
There is no point, I know that.

Well, I think it's bad
Yes I know that for a fact
Well goodbye for now.

Alice Gillies (9)
Woodbury Salterton CE Primary, Woodbury Salterton

Habitats

H abitats destroyed

A nimals with no homes

B urning habitats

I nsects dying

T rees falling

A nimals are losing homes

T his needs to stop

S top!

Joff Rorke (10)

Woodbury Salterton CE Primary, Woodbury Salterton

Our Earth Environment

The Earth is dying
We need to stop this right now
Our world is in danger
It's a disastrous mess -
Help!

Kyle Johnston (11)
Woodbury Salterton CE Primary, Woodbury Salterton

213

Animals

Tigers stripy
Monkeys loud
Deer with antlers
Squirrels with tails
All animals are unique.

Frank Rorke (8)

Woodbury Salterton CE Primary, Woodbury Salterton

Save Rhinos

A haiku

Rhinos are dying
We must save them now or else
People get their horns.

Henry Haines (11)

Woodbury Salterton CE Primary, Woodbury Salterton

YOUNG WRITERS INFORMATION

We hope you have enjoyed reading this book – and that you will continue to in the coming years.

If you're the parent or family member of an enthusiastic poet or story writer, do visit our website **www.youngwriters.co.uk/subscribe** and sign up to receive news, competitions, writing challenges and tips, activities and much, much more! There's lots to keep budding writers motivated!

If you would like to order further copies of this book, or any of our other titles, then please give us a call or order via your online account.

Young Writers
Remus House
Coltsfoot Drive
Peterborough
PE2 9BF
(01733) 890066
info@youngwriters.co.uk

Join in the conversation!
Tips, news, giveaways and much more!

 YoungWritersUK   YoungWritersCW   youngwriterscw

Scan me to watch The Big Green video!